Ghosts of Santa Clara County

By Aubrey Graves

Photos by Aubrey Graves

(Unless Otherwise Noted)

DEADication

This book is dedicated to my sister-in-law Jen.

Table of Contents

Great America, Santa Clara, CA

Ghosts of Santa Clara County

Introduction

Originated in 1850, Santa Clara County is claimed to be haunted by numerous restless spirits. This book covers many of the well known haunts around the county, as well as a few others I found in my research. The stories included consist of legend and lore based on different individuals' personal paranormal experiences and opinions.

Stanford Mausoleum, photo by Sean Parola

Hecker Pass

The ghost of a young woman in a red dress has been seen walking along Hecker Pass (Highway 152) for generations by several witnesses. She is known to hitch rides from taxi drivers. They all claim they pick her up, and that she then vanishes suddenly. One cab driver from Watsonville had an experience with the ghost in the red dress, not knowing she was a spirit until the following day. It began one night at around midnight. The taxi driver was near Mt. Madonna when a beautiful young woman waved him down and asked for a ride. Contemplating whether to give the lady a ride at such a late hour, he decided to take the woman to her destination. She asked to stop near the bottom of Hecker Pass Hill, next to a house that stood alone. He said he felt her become nervous as they approached the home. The spirit suddenly jumped out of the car and bolted toward the house, not paying her charge for the cab ride.

The next day, the cab driver went to the residence he had seen the young woman run into the night before. An elderly woman opened the door and he began telling her what had happened the previous evening and described the young woman in the red dress. The homeowner picked up a framed photo of her two daughters and showed it to the taxi driver. He immediately recognized the young lady and pointed her out. Shocked, the mother then replied that her daughter had died in a car accident years before as she was heading home. She offered to pay the cab driver but he insisted that she keep the money.

Hecker Pass, Gilroy / Watsonville, CA

Location:

Hecker Pass (Hwy 152)

Gilroy / Watsonville, CA

Mount Madonna

Sarah Miller's spirit has been seen around Mt. Madonna since her death on June 14, 1879. The land was owned by her father Henry Miller "The Cattle King," one of Gilroy's founders who had purchased it only months before his daughter died. One hot summer day, 8-year-old Sarah was riding her trusty steed back to her family's campsite. Suddenly, her horse tripped, which made Sarah fall and break her neck. Since then, hundreds of witnesses have alleged seeing a ghostly apparition on horseback riding along the mountainside or riding in the back seat of their cars. Legend has it that Sarah is known to get into people's cars, trying to hitch a ride and find her way off the mountain, where she's believed to be trapped for eternity.

Miller Mansion Ruins, Mount Madonna, Gilroy/ Watsonville, CA

The Author's husband, Sean at the Miller Mansion Ruins

Sarah Miller, late 1870s, public domain photo

Sarah is also believed to haunt the Mt. Madonna Inn on top of the mountain. Visitors have seen and heard a horse trotting and galloping around the Inn, along with seeing lights turn on and off late at night, when no one was in the building. In recent years, a Park Ranger claimed to have heard a young woman screaming for help from the Mt. Madonna Inn. He searched the perimeter of the building and couldn't find anyone. Henry Miller's spirit has been seen and sensed as well over the years.

Additional Information:
- Recently, some campers awoke in the morning on Mt. Madonna to find horse tracks and small human footprints circling their tent.

Location:
7850 Pole Line Road
Gilroy/ Watsonville, CA

Pacheco Pass (Highway 152)

Over the centuries, numerous deaths have occurred on and around "Blood Alley" creating its dark history. It is alleged that Indians were massacred by where the highway now lies. This, along with many other events and accidents that occurred at this site is believed to have created a residual energy to forever repeat itself. Some claim that "it's almost a Bermuda Triangle on land. People have said to see ghosts that are dressed as if they lived as far back as the 1700s. There have been reports of Indians, soldiers and settlers on wagons witnessed along Pacheco Pass. Many people have seen a man believed to be a Franciscan Monk and described him wearing a black robe and standing on the side of the road, between Casa De Fruta and Bell's Station. Others have reported seeing a headless man walking on the side of Pacheco Pass near Bolsa Road.

Witnesses claim to have seen a hitchhiking ghost around the area. The young girl dressed in jeans and a plaid shirt, which now haunts the vicinity, was tragically hit by a semi-truck while trying to hitch a ride long ago. It is alleged by various truck drivers that they pulled over to give the phantom hitchhiker a ride, and spoke with the ghost, whom they believed to be alive. As she would walk around the truck to the passenger door, she'd suddenly vanish.

In a small grove of rocks off the highway near the mission, the ghost of a woman has been seen on occasion late at night. She appears in her wedding dress in the vicinity that allegedly her fiancé died in from a car wreck. After his death, the ghost bride took her life by jumping off the rocks, hoping to join her love once again.

Pacheco Pass can be upsetting or frightening to some sensitives or psychics. Sylvia Browne is one such person. Browne claimed to receive psychic images there, and said she saw "a little girl in a covered wagon cowering with her fists pressed against her eyes while Indians raged around the wagon train. Her sense of hopelessness was overwhelming," (quote from *Haunted Houses of California*.)

Additional Information:

-   The ghost of a woman in a Victorian dress has been sighted along the road. It is alleged that she's endlessly searching for her child.
-   Some people claim to have anxiety when driving through Hwy 152, while others reported feeling distorted or unexplained fright.

Location:
Highway 152, the highway connecting Watsonville and Gilroy
Santa Clara County, CA

Coggeshall Mansion

Once a residence, funeral parlor and a restaurant, the beautiful Victorian on 115 N Santa Cruz Ave was constructed in 1891 for the Coggeshall family. Lots of paranormal activity has been experienced on the property and it is alleged that it is haunted by a little girl, believed to be the daughter of the Coggeshalls. The ghost is often seen in the cupola, and occasionally near the entrance inside the mansion.

The Coggeshall Mansion, Los Gatos, CA

While the Coggeshall Mansion was used as a restaurant under the name Trevese, the bartender claimed to have received prank phone calls on his cell phone. He noticed from his caller I.D. that the number which kept calling him, belonged to the restaurant. The bartender quickly ran upstairs to see who was calling, but no one was there. The bartender had another eerie experience one evening when he was closing up for the night, but first had to run an errand. He returned to the mansion to find that all the candles on every table had been lit. The restaurant was still locked when the incident occurred.

Additional Information:

- One evening a cook stacked plates on a shelf and left the kitchen for a moment. When he returned, he found that the stacked plates had been moved across the shelf.

- Light footsteps have been heard and champagne bottles have been rearranged on their own.

Location:

115 N. Santa Cruz Avenue

Los Gatos, CA

Green Valley Disposal Company

The office of the Disposal Company is run in an old house, and claimed to be occupied by a ghost by the name of Julius. It is said that strange unexplainable occurrences occur often throughout the house, almost on a daily basis. Cold spots have been felt in certain rooms, even without the possibility of their having been caused by drafts or a problem with the heating system.

Upstairs, there have been claims of the drawers of filing cabinets opening and closing on their own at a rapid pace. Allegedly, during the night you can hear what sounds like an office chair rolling around on hard wood floors, even though the upstairs is completely carpeted.

Julius the ghost is known to play with electrical appliances on the property as well. After the company had a new phone system installed, it completely shut down with no explanation. Engineers were baffled. Calls that were on hold would disconnect and only Julius was to blame. One employee claimed to have seen his electric calculator being typed on by an unseen force, as it sat on his desk.

Location:

644 N Santa Cruz Ave

Los Gatos, CA

Highway 17

Highway 17 is known to be one of the most dangerous roads in California. The 26-mile winding route travels through the mountains from Los Gatos to Scotts Valley, California. For generations, many drivers and passengers have reported seeing apparitions walking or standing along the highway and even sitting in the back seats of cars. Others have claimed to see white vaporous clouds floating over the lanes. Many witnesses have also seen what looked to be solid bodies lying on the side of the road, covered in blood. Along with seeing spirits wander the area, visitors driving through sharp turns have heard sounds of collisions and tires screeching to a halt, without the presence of any accidents or reckless drivers.

Additional Information:
-   An apparition of an Ohlone Indian man has been seen for centuries walking on the side of the highway. Legend has it he is the cause of all the accidents.

Location:
The windy section of Highway 17 between Los Gatos and Scotts Valley, CA

The Lavender Lady

The beautiful Victorian on Tait Street in Los Gatos is said to be haunted by a gentle female spirit. The home was built in 1889. In 2003, it was purchased by Lynley Kerr Hogan, who became aware of the paranormal activity in the place and soon after named it The Lavender Lady. She and her three daughters have seen dark shadows from within the structure, and heard unexplainable sounds and footsteps, caused by the Lavender Lady's ghost.

One evening, Lynley invited the ghost to dinner.

"As soon as I ended the question, I immediately saw a dark shadow come from out of the wall right in front of me. To me she's saying yes, yes, yes," said Lynley, quote from a GPS video.

Her apparition disappeared before her very eyes soon after. In 2010, a construction worker said he felt something brush up against him in the cellar. The Lavender Lady's soft presence is not a bother to anyone, but it's a mystery as to why her spirit still resides in the mature home.

Sensitive and Paranormal Investigator Nancy Bowman and her ghost hunting team Global Paranormal Society (GPS) investigated the residence on October 29, 2011. GPS discovered high EMF in the center of the living room and could not find an explanation other than it being paranormal. Karen Casella Adamski, sensitive, paranormal investigator and dowsing rod specialist from GPS, also saw "a light-colored foggy shadow" in one of the bedrooms while touring the house.

Karen began using dowsing rods to attempt to communicate with the ghost who resided in the home. Right away the rods began moving by an unseen force, and crossed for a *Yes* answer when asked if she was speaking with the Lavender Lady. Sensitive and paranormal investigator Bela from GPS sensed the ghost was once a servant in the home, and when asked the rods immediately crossed for *Yes* once again.

Lynley wanted to know if the spirit approved of the name the Lavender Lady ... she did. As Lynley started to cry in joy and amazement, she asked the ghost if she knew how much she enjoys having her there. The rods crossed with a big *Yes*.

"Did you know the family before they moved here?"

The dowsing rods quickly opened for *No*.

"Are you stuck here?"

The rods opened with another *no* response.

Bela also sensed that the spirit died while giving child birth. When asked, the spirit crossed the rods. After a series of questions, they found out that the ghost of the woman who resides in the home died in the 1930s.

A friend of Lynley's who visits the home regularly brought the Lavender Lady a music box as an offering and a token of his affection for her. After announcing that he had brought it for her, the K-2 Meter immediately started to light up. As the music box started to play, the K-2 meter began blinking.

GPS then began using the Ghost box to try and communicate further.

"Could you say one of our names?" asked Nancy.

A voice then said, "Edward," which was Lynley's friend's name.

Nancy went on...

"How many people are here?"

A voice responded saying, "Seven." There were, in all, seven people in the home at the time.

"What is your name?"

"Lisa," was then said very loud and clear, in a female voice.

"Are you here to help Lynley," an investigator asked.

"I love her," said a female voice from the spirit box.

Location:

230 Tait Avenue

Los Gatos, CA

(408) 316-4750

www.thelavenderladyoflosgatos.com

Oak Meadow Park

The 12-acre park, established in 1958 is claimed to be haunted by several ghosts. Both the W.E. Bill Mason Carousel and the Billy Jones Wildcat Railroad are said to have plenty of paranormal activity.

The historic carousel was built in England in 1910, and then shipped to America where it was moved around for many years to different locations. The present executive administrator of the carousel claims that strange, unexplained events occur around it after hours. Gates have been seen and heard opening and closing on their own. The carousel bell that sounds when the ride begins is said to ring randomly when the machine is shut down, and lights turn on by themselves. Some believe a former devoted volunteer by the name of Paul Seaborn, who died in 1990, haunts the ride.

The Wildcat Railroad was built by William "Billy" Jones in 1941. The miniature tracks and steam engine wound through Jones' property until it was moved to the park in 1969, one year after he passed away. Jones' tall ghostly apparition has been seen wearing coveralls and a big smile, standing in front of the water tower near the tracks.

Location:
200 Blossom Hill Road
Los Gatos, CA

The Opera House

The Los Gatos Opera House, built in 1904, is known for its ghostly photos taken throughout the years. The most well-known of these photos was printed in the Los Gatos Weekly Times in 1992. The photographer took about two dozen pictures of an employee and noticed that in two of the photos there was a shadow-figure standing in the background on the right-hand balcony. Years later, another photographer who was taking photos of the outside of the building caught the ghostly apparition of a woman peering out the 2nd story window.

Some employees claim that the Opera House, now used for wedding receptions and events, is haunted by a woman who has been heard and seen by countless people, who is believed to be the spirit captured in photographs. One staff member became a true believer when she tried to sneak out before her shift was over. As she tried to leave, the door wouldn't budge and she was locked in until the end of her shift. The spirit has a reputation to being ethical and is protective over the Opera House in a kind manor.

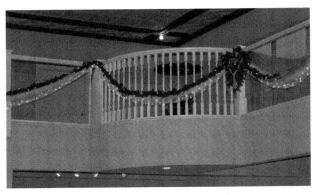

The balcony where the ghost was captured on film, the Opera House, Los Gatos, CA

I spoke with a current employee at the Opera House, who said they named the ghost Elizabeth. She exclaimed, "I personally haven't had an encounter with her, but I do believe she's here."

Location:
140 West Main Street
Los Gatos, CA

Village Lane

Built over several lost graves of the old Los Gatos Cemetery; Village Lane is known to display lots of paranormal activity. In 1890, the city decided to expand the cemetery, so they moved it to another location. They tried contacting family members of the deceased to ask their permission to move their loved ones' graves, but some were never found and others refused to rebury the graves. Some people believe the spirits of some of the bodies buried underneath the new structures are responsible for the haunting and strange events that occur occasionally.

It is said that in some of the stores mirrors will tilt and door bells will ring when no one is around. Strange noises have been heard throughout Village Lane including radios turning on and blasting music by themselves. Double D's Sports Bar on Village Lane is allegedly the most haunted business on North Santa Cruz Avenue. There have been claims of cold spots, random gusts of wind and apparitions witnessed. Some have reported feeling as if someone was looking over their shoulder.

Additional Information:

- A ghost woman has been witnessed by several people walking through the shops.

- Local ghost hunters claim that Village Lane is haunted by the spirit of a young boy named Willie, who died of Pneumonia in 1889 and was buried near Double D's.

Location:

North Santa Cruz Avenue

Los Gatos, CA

The Marsh Road Ravine

On November 3, 1981, 14-year-old Marcy Renee Conrad was tragically murdered by her peer, 16-year-old Anthony Jacques Broussard. Broussard dumped Conrad's deceased body near a ravine off Marsh Road in Milpitas. Broussard went to school that day and bragged to his friends about the horrific things he had done to Marcy Conrad and urged his friends to come see the body.

Strangely, car loads of teens went to go view Conrad lifelessly lying half naked in the leaves. The case wasn't reported for over 2 days. Many locals were disgusted, disappointed and shocked about Conrad's friends and peers not contacting authorities sooner.

It is said that Marcy Conrad haunts the ravine off Marsh Road. She has been witnessed by many individuals near the bridge at night. Drivers claim to see Conrad's ghost in the rear-view mirror, and as they look back she vanishes. Electronic devices are known to get drained quickly and die underneath the bridge at night.

The tragedy is what inspired the movie, *River's Edge* (1986), starring Keanu Reeves and Crispin Glover.

Location:

Marsh Road

Milpitas, CA

A Milpitas Residence

I interviewed Lucy Rucchio, who used to live in a haunted house in Milpitas, California for nine years starting back in 1977. Not long after she moved into the home, she began to have frightening paranormal encounters. One day, a little blonde-haired girl in a pink jumper walked past Lucy in the hallway.

"I saw a small child walk across the hall from my bedroom … I thought, now how could my daughter get out of the bathtub and walk down the hall? She hadn't taken her first steps yet."

Lucy quickly ran back to the bathroom to find her daughter still in the tub. It was then that she realized that her home was haunted.

"After I had realized I had seen a spirit, I freaked out, dressed my daughter quickly and went to my mother's."

Lucy explained her uncanny encounter to her mom as soon as she arrived at her home.

"When I told her what happened, my mother then announced that she too had seen the little girl at my house on several occasions."

She hadn't told Lucy about her sightings because she was afraid it would just frighten her.

Lucy's next paranormal encounter took place in her living room, where a fire was constantly burning, but it was always still so cold. While sitting down on the sofa, she looked up to see a hanging ceiling plant "Spinning like a top."

"Time went by, and my fear diminished. I never saw the little girl again, but strange things were still happening in the house," Lucy explained.

Many times she'd notice her daughter playing with an unseen force, almost as if a child were sitting beside her, babbling and giggling. As soon as Lucy would enter the room, her daughter would immediately be silent and stop playing.

Lucy decided to ask her landlord if she knew any of the history of the home and if someone had ever died there. Her landlord told her that the 40s Spanish-style house was once owned by a family by the name of Graves, and that their 2-year-old daughter tragically died in the house.

Location:
A private residence
Milpitas, CA

Pacific Palms Grill and Bar

The building where Pacific Palms is located was once a restaurant called Das Gasthaus, which opened in 1980. A previous owner by the name of Carl Hacke, is said to have devoted his life to the restaurant before he was relieved of his position by his business partners. Chef Carl was reputed to have a great sense of humor. Sometimes during open hours he'd wear his WWII helmet and blow his bugle for his customers' entertainment, filling the restaurant with laughter. He loved Das Gasthaus, and after he became uninvolved with the restaurant he was never the same. Years later Carl died a poor man.

Soon after Hacke's death, paranormal activity began to occur in the building. Owners at the time claimed to hear pots and pans rattle on their own during after hours. Both owners said they saw the ghost of a man that fit Carl Hacke's description in the kitchen on separate occasions. It is believed that Carl's spirit now inhabits Pacific Palms Grill and Bar. Nothing could keep the devoted chef away from the building of his former restaurant, not even death itself.

Location:
1380 S Main Street
Milpitas, CA

The Rengstorff House

The Rengstorff House was built in 1867 by Henry Rengstorff, one of the founding fathers of Mountain View. He resided there with his wife and seven children, until he died in the home in 1906. After Rengstorff's wife passed in 1919, the home was occupied by their daughter Elise, her husband and her orphaned nephew. Years later, Elise died in the home and the Crump family bought the Victorian in the 60s.

Henry Rengstroff, founding father of Mountain View, courtesy of the Rengstroff House

As soon as the Crump family moved into the house, they alleged hearing a child cry in the night, as well as thumping noises on the stairs.

Mr. Crump stated, "Finally I just came to believe that there was something in the house that I couldn't understand," (Palo Alto Times article). One day, friends of the family stopped by the residence to find no one home, but saw the front door knob turning on its own.

The Rengstroff House, Mountain View, CA

After the Crump family moved away, the home remained vacant for years. During the time of vacancy, several people who passed by reported witnessing a young woman looking out of the upstairs window.

In Antoinette May's book titled *"Haunted Houses and Wandering Ghosts of Califonia,* she writes, "A series of tenants and neighbors have reported unexplainable manifestations.

The sounds of crying late at night, lights that flash on and off and uncanny cold drafts."

Famous psychic Sylvia Browne from Campbell, California investigated the home and had several psychic impressions of the houses' past. Browne believes one man was strangled to death over money on the second floor. She also envisioned an angry old man with one leg in a wheelchair. There is no proof through the family's history that these events occurred, but that doesn't mean it didn't happen.

The Rengstorff House, located on Stierlin Road, stood dilapidated and condemned before the historical quarters was moved to its present location on North Shorline Boulevard. In 1991, after being restored and refurbished, it opened to the public for tours, receptions, parties and events. Today the reports of the crying and the thumping continue, along with the apparition of the young woman in the window.

Additional Information:

- Mysteriously a secret room was found in the attic, in later years, with a hospital bed and leather restraining cuffs.

Location:
3070 North Shoreline Boulevard
Mountain View, CA

Stanford University

Leland and Jane Stanford lost their beloved son Leland Jr. at the ripe age of fifteen, from Typhoid fever on March 13, 1884; exactly 100 years to the day of my birth. Unable to cope with Leland Junior's unexpected departure, the Stanfords held a number of séances trying to make contact with their son after his death. Leland Stanford claimed that his son's ghost appeared to him one night during a séance. It is said that Leland Jr. asked his father to dedicate his life to founding a university.

Leland and Jane Stanford, courtesy of Wikipedia

~ 40 ~

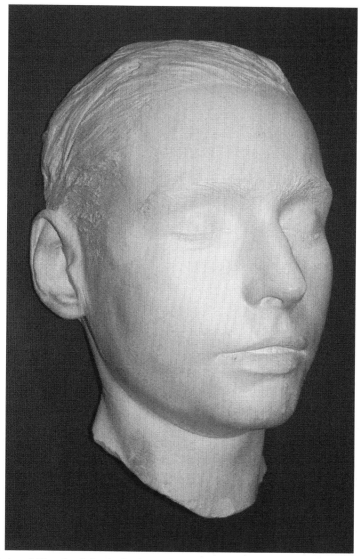

Leland Stanford Junior's death mask, Leland Junior Museum, Palo Alto, CA

~ 41 ~

Leland took his paranormal experience and his deceased son's request very seriously. Within a year Leland and Jane founded Stanford University, where they all are now laid to rest. The Stanford family gravesite is in the extravagant mausoleum located on the corner of Campus Drive and Palm Drive at the historical college. Before being laid in his final resting spot, Leland Jr. was buried adjacent to the memorial, with a large headstone engraved with a poem that read:

MUST I NOT HEAR WHAT
THOU HEAREST NOT,
TROUBLING THE AIR OF
THIS SUNNY SPOT?
IS THERE NOT SOMETHING
TO NONE BUT ME,
TOLD BY THE RUSTLING
OF EVERY TREE?

SONG HAS BEEN HERE WITH
ITS FLOW OF THOUGHT,
LOVE WITH ITS PASSIONATE
VISIONS FRAUGHT,
DEATH BREATHING STILLNESS
AND SADNESS AROUND
AND IS IT NOT, IS IT NOT
HAUNTED GROUND?

YES IT IS HAUNTED, THIS
QUIET SCENE,
FAIR AS IT LOOKS
AND ALL SOFTLY GREEN,
YET FEAR THOU NOT, FOR
THE SPELL IS THROWN
AND THE MIGHT OF THE SHADOWS
ON ME ALONE.

HAVE I NOT UNDER
THESE WHISPERING LEAVES
WOVEN SUCH DREAMS
AS YOUNG HAPPY HEART WEAVES
SHADOWS UNTO WHICH
LIFE SEEMS BOUND
AND IS IT NOT, IS IT NOT
HAUNTED GROUND?
-Felicia Dorthea Hemans, 1824

Mr. Stanford died on June 21st, 1893, from heart failure at age sixty-nine. Mrs. Stanford passed away when she was seventy-seven, from strychnine poisoning on February 28th, 1905. According to various articles, the Stanford mausoleum and museum are haunted by Mrs. Stanford's restless spirit. Several eyewitnesses have claimed to see her ghost in the area for over a century. Could she be endlessly searching for her beloved son? Or maybe she has unfinished business? Some believe Jane Stanford was murdered and her poisoning was intentional. If this were the case, it's logical that she'd haunt the vicinity, waiting for someone to hear her story and obtain justice ..."and is it not haunted ground?"

The Stanford Mausoleum, Stanford University, Palo Alto, CA

Jane Stanford, courtesy of Wikipedia

The Hoover Tower, located on the University's campus, is believed to be haunted as well. The historic structure was founded in 1941 by the 31st President of the United States, Herbert Hoover. Before being elected as president, Hoover spent many years of his life at Stanford earning his degree in mining engineering and geology. He named the tower The Hoover Institution of War and Peace, devoting it to the advanced study of economics, political economy and politics.

President Herbert Hoover, 1928, courtesy of Wikipedia

It is claimed that President Herbert Hoover's faithful spirit has haunted the tower since his death on October 20th, 1964. He has been witnessed by several individuals wearing a pinstripe suit and a frown on his face. He is said to be bald and looks middle aged.

~ 46 ~

The Herbert Hoover Tower, Stanford University, Palo Alto, CA

According to Jeff Dwyer's book *Ghost Hunter's Guide to the San Francisco Bay Area*, the spirit of a young college student has been witnessed walking in a hurry, carrying books and dressed in 20s or 30s attire near the Hoover Tower. "I'm late!" he exclaimed to an individual one evening before disappearing.

Location:
701 Welch Rd #3328
Palo Alto, CA

Emerson Street

From 1986 to 1992, Karen Holman, the past president of Palo Alto Stanford Heritage, lived in a haunted house on Emerson Street in Palo Alto. Shortly after she and her husband moved into the old home, they began noticing unusual occurrences on a daily basis. Every evening, the smell of cigarette smoke permeated from the same room of the house, although neither Karen nor her husband smoked. Every night before bed, their dog would enter the smelly room and would bark with its hackles raised. At times the Holmans both felt as if they were being watched by an unseen force that gave off an eerie vibe.

Another home on the 500 block of Emerson Street is claimed to be so haunted, that it caused a family to move in recent years. Unexplainable voices and footsteps were heard in the home's hallway. Doors slammed, pipes banged "with a haunting rhythm," and lights turned on in the middle of the night.

Location:
Emerson Street
Palo Alto, CA

Century 25

The old 60s theater is said to be haunted after multiple paranormal experiences occurred throughout the building. It is claimed that a former employee hung herself in the projection booth and now haunts the vicinity. When a staff member was starting the projector one evening, a wrench was thrown at him by an unseen force. A voice of a woman has also been heard singing and talking near the projector on various occasions. Cold spots have been felt in the booth, and it would get so chilly at times, you could see your breath.

The ghost of a woman has been witnessed walking through the lobby and out to the parking lot where she vanishes suddenly. A previous employee reported talking to the spirit of a girl, not knowing she was a ghost. Noticing a picture of the girl on the theater wall, she asked another staff member, who told her that the ghost she spoke with had died years earlier. People claimed to see the spirit of a lady sitting down in the theater. As soon as the movie starts, she is said to get up, walk down the aisle and disappear.

In the theater, seats have been seen moving on their own, as if someone was pushing weight down and sitting on them. Growling noises have been heard behind the screen, along with random uncanny occurrences, making Century 25 one of the most haunted theaters in the county.

Additional Information:

- While an employee was sitting in the projection room where a woman allegedly took her life, she witnessed the door opening and closing on its own.

- It is claimed that the left theater is the area with the most paranormal activity.

Location:

1694 Saratoga Ave

San Jose, CA

Chuck E. Cheese's

The two-story Chuck E. Cheese's (once King Norman's Toy Store) on Tully Road in San Jose is said to be haunted by two children. The first child, who has been witnessed by several people, is a little girl who allegedly fell from the toy store's third-level loft and died. The ghost of the little girl has been witnessed peering out of the window of the third story, which is closed for the public, ever since her heart-wrenching death. Her apparition has been seen by many, and even was captured on film. It is said that when trying to close up for the night, employees will sometimes turn around to find tables unexplainably set for a party of 6.

Chuck E. Cheese's, San Jose, CA

The other ghost said to haunt the vicinity is the spirit of a 3-year-old boy who was said to have fallen down the stairs, breaking his neck. During after hours, employees of Chuck E. Cheese's said they have heard a toddler crying for his mother, when there's no one around accountable for it. An employee commented, "To this day when the C.E.C. cast is closing, the tick tock ride powers on and starts by itself."

Chuck E. Cheese's, San Jose, CA

Location:

2445 Fontaine Road

San Jose, CA

The Grant House

Nestled in the foothills of Joseph D. Grant County Park stands a beautiful Victorian home built in 1882. The haunted house was owned and occupied by the Grant Family for generations until it was bought by the county and opened as a museum and the park's headquarters. What brought the house to be haunted where the murders which took place on the land.

One of Joseph's daughters named Edith was said to be a homicidal maniac. It was pronounced that in the 1930s she shot two trespassers who were riding on her land. Almost a year later she shot a man in a bar after a disagreement. People claim that Edith spent most of her life confined to her room because of her insanity. She was never sent to jail or a mental facility because it was said in both cases, that the sheriff claimed it was self-defense.

Years later Edith had a baby girl and her older sister Josephine took custody after knowing what Edith was capable (and not capable) of doing. Sadly, a couple years later Josephine died and some believe she was murdered by her sister. Edith was given back her baby, who tragically died from a gunshot wound less than a year later.

It is believed that the home is haunted by either Edith or Josephine and maybe even a few other spirits as well. Over the course of the next years, many people reported hearing footsteps, doors slamming and the sound of furniture being thrown around.

Some visitors have claimed to see apparitions moving throughout the house as well as being touched by an unseen force. It is alleged that some people have been pushed out the door when trying to enter or leave the murderess' bedroom. Several women have claimed to feel their hair being pulled or to have felt a hand on their shoulder while standing in Edith's room. A historian claimed that a medium held a séance at the Grant house, and that during the channeling she tried to take her own life by attempting to jump out the window.

Additional Information:

- Dark moving shadows have been spotted on and around the property along with flashes of light.

- EVPs and possible spirit orbs have been caught on location.

Location:

18405 Mount Hamilton Road

San Jose, CA

The Hill Park House

My first paranormal experience took place in San Jose at the home I was raised in and lived in until I was thirteen years old. The activity in the house was subtle for years and slowly escalated after it was acknowledged, especially after a Ouija board was used by me and my friends. Random objects in the home would go missing and then appear in the strangest spots, sometimes months later. We would experience minor disturbances at times, such as the sounds of footsteps in the dining room and in my parents' bedroom, doors slamming and lights flickering at various times. Water faucets would turn on randomly. One particular occasion I will never forget was when my friend Jennifer, my parents, and I were all awakened at 3 o'clock one morning by the water faucet in the bathtub turning on full blast. We all got to the bathroom at the same time to see what was going on. None of us had an explanation for what had occurred.

Soon afterwards, my Sister-in-law Jen came forward with her encounter that had just taken place while she was staying with me when my parents were out of town. She told me that the night before, while lying in my mom's bed asleep, she was awakened by something which felt like a finger tapping her shoulder. She turned around expecting to see me or her daughter, but no one was there. Jen decided to get up and investigate to see if I was just playing a trick on her, but she found us sound asleep. After explaining her experience she exclaimed, "This place is *so* haunted!"

It got even more bizarre a few days later when I was over at my neighbor David's house, and out of nowhere he started telling me how he thought his house was occupied by a ghost. He said that really weird things had been happening recently, and that he had just had an uncanny experience the night before. David described the same encounter Jen had experienced. He had also gotten out of bed to see if his partner had tapped his shoulder, but David found him passed out in the living room.

When I told Dave that Jen had just had the same eerie incident a few days prior, he asked me if we'd encountered other supernatural occurrences in our home, because he had witnessed an abundant amount in his. David said that on a couple of occasions he'd seen everything on his night stand slide off onto the ground. He also claimed having heard strange sounds and witnessing a dark apparition moving about his living room late at night. Conveniently, Dave was friends with a few psychics who came to the house and knew right away that there an angry spirit haunting the vicinity. All three psychics said they felt that a horrific event had taken place around a century earlier, on David's property and on ours. Two of the psychics claimed that a teenage boy around the age of 18 or 19 had killed his 3 sisters between the two properties. After taking their innocent lives, he hanged himself in the vicinity. David's psychic friends believe the boy's evil spirit still lingers in the area trying to create havoc whenever possible.

Not knowing what evil a spirit board could bring in, I thought it would be a cool way to try and communicate with the ghost. When my friends and I first tried to use the Ouija board, it didn't work properly, and we were unable to communicate with whatever supernatural force dwelled in the house. It was almost a year later when I tried again and received messages from beyond.

I asked the spirit if it died on the property long ago and the curser glided slowly over "Yes." Making contact and receiving a response, I continued with my next question, asking what its name was. Amazingly "W-I-L-B-E-R-T - F-R-O-S-T" was spelled out. My mouth dropped in disbelief. It wasn't until that moment that I believed spirit boards could actually work.

After becoming aware of the fact that our house was haunted and having spoken to the spirit by name, I started to notice more unusual activity. At first it seemed innocent, but as time went on the ghost seemed more and more to be trying to scare and upset me. It was usually at night that the malicious activity occurred. Some nights I'd lie in bed trying to sleep, scared and paralyzed with fright. I'd notice a dark shadow hovering over my bed on the ceiling. At first I thought it was my imagination, until I saw my cat looking straight up at the supernatural force in discomfort. During two events, I saw the outline of the spirit standing in the dark corner behind my bedroom door. It scared me so badly that I'd just hide under the covers and cry myself to sleep.

On one occasion my friend Becky and I were home alone for the night and both witnessed the ghost boy's apparition standing in front of my mom's bathroom window. There were loud footsteps and bangs, almost like furniture was being moved around and dropped onto the hardwood floor, coming from the vicinity. The light flickered the entire time the paranormal activity was occurring. The moment the activity began, my friend and I were more scared than we'd ever been before. It felt like something straight out of a horror flick. After several minutes, of watching in shock, we unexpectedly heard a knock at the front door. It was our neighbor David checking in on us to make sure we were alright.

"How did you know we were scared?" I asked.

"Weird stuff was just happening at my house as well, and I was curious to see if you also were experiencing anything," he replied.

It was 1997 and our last year of living on Hill Park Drive when my friends and I had another supernatural experience. Mitchell, Jennifer and I decided to try and communicate with the spirit once again. I was very hesitant, since it seemed to come around more frequently and viciously at that point. But Mitchell was skeptical, so being the adolescent I was, I felt I had to prove my allegations. While communicating with the ghost boy on the spirit board, we suddenly started smelling smoke. We looked up to find the sheet covering the stand-up lamp on fire. That exact sheet had been on the lamp for months and had never gotten hot enough to start a fire until then. My mom finally started to become a believer after that particular incident, which she agreed was just too weird to ignore. She took my Ouija board, and broke it over her knee, and threw it in the trash. She told me to never bring anything like that in her house again.

That was not the only time an unusual fire had occurred in the area. Earlier that year David went out into the garage to start his car. It started smoking and quickly burst into flames. It ended up burning down the garage, the kitchen and the dining room, destroying the house by the heat and smoke. David couldn't help but wonder if the horrible event that could have taken his life was caused by something paranormal.

Recently, my husband and I stopped by the old Hill Park House, and it was up for sale again. As I was walking across the street and approaching the property, my EMF detector began to spike for a few seconds. I wondered if it was caused by something paranormal. I looked around and noticed there were no power lines above or near me. Standing in front of the house I grew up in was haunting in itself. So many memories...and so many nights I was scared to death. I finally have closure, I thought. I said aloud in a low tone, "I just wanted you to know how much you scared me when I was younger. You had a big effect on me." As I started to walk away from the house, the EMF Detector spiked high in another area, this time for about eight seconds.

My EMF Detector picking up high electromagnetic field in front of the property on Hill Park Drive, San Jose, CA

The Hill Park House was definitely strange at times. I truly believe the ghost's bad energy influenced my family to do certain things that they wouldn't normally do. I still wonder how our lives would be different if we hadn't lived there. One thing's for sure: I wouldn't have written this book, or have this crazy story to tell if we had lived somewhere else.

The author standing in her home on Halloween, 1988, notice bizarre glowing streak on her left

- A photo expert does not believe the streak on the photo on the previous page was an error on film, and was unable to give me an answer to why it's in the photograph.

- Two psychics who had never met said they saw a spirit standing near me. One of the psychics claimed to see many faces below.

Additional Information:

- I'd frequently see things moving from the corner of my eye, usually in the hallway.

- When I was younger, I had a recorder that would pick up a strange young male voice that sounded very livid, and once it even yelled. It frightened me so badly; I stopped using the recorder after that.

Location:

A private residence on Hill Park Drive

San Jose, CA

The Holiday Inn

It is claimed that in 1980, a man checked into room 538 at the former LeBaron Hotel, to "meet his maker." He took his own life by overdosing on pills and people say that his spirit still occupies the room. Unexplainable sadness is felt in room 538 along with the feeling of uncanny energy. It is said that water faucets turn on and off by themselves and the elevator gets hijacked by the spirits occasionally. Maids claim that many times when they use the elevator, it stops on the fifth floor, where the death occurred, when it wasn't selected to stop there. A majority of previous employees try to avoid the fifth floor, especially after having an encounter with the spirit. A maid claimed she felt her hair being pulled and also heard her name being softly whispered in her ear while cleaning room 538 one day.

Location:
1350 N 1st Street
San Jose, CA

Oak Hill Memorial Cemetery

The historic Oak Hill Cemetery was the very first official graveyard in California. In 1839, people were given permission to bury their loved ones near a tree on the property. As time went on the population of the deceased grew there until it was established by the city as Oak Hill Memorial Park in 1958.

It is said that "Almost every night you can see the ghost of a man walking around the cemetery" (*Haunts of San Jose.)* Many security guards claim to hear disembodied voices and see shadow-like apparitions in the mausoleum. One staff member claimed to have heard a baby crying in the vicinity and to have seen ghosts of children playing while working the graveyard shift. Security guards are said to resign often due to the frequency with which the paranormal activity occurs there.

Oak Hill Memorial Cemetery, San Jose, CA

Additional Information:

- A mortician claimed that an ice-cold finger poked his spine while he was preparing for a burial.

Location:

300 Curtner Avenue

San Jose, CA

The Old Spaghetti Factory

The Old Spaghetti Factory in San Jose has been claimed to be haunted over the years. The restaurant started operating in 1969. Unfortunately, I was unable to find any history on the place, other than it being allegedly haunted.

Recently, a group of psychics were dining at the restaurant and witnessed the ghost of a little girl walking around their table. On another occasion, a sensitive claimed to see a little girl hovering over him and his dinner party. Eerie growling sounds have been heard in the dining room by visitors, along with an uncanny long-winded, 'Booooo.'

One night when the staff was locking up for the night, the video games in the loft started turning off by themselves. There also have been claims of items being misplaced or moved. Staff members will return the next day to see that the cooking supplies have been rearranged.

Location:
51 N San Pedro Street
San Jose, CA

The Rosicrucian Egyptian Museum

Founded in 1915, the Rosicrucian Egyptian Museum is definitely a place where the veils are very thin. Both ancient and vintage apparitions have been witnessed, as well as shadow people. Disembodied voices and footsteps have been heard, and items have disappeared. Many visitors and past employees had claimed they felt as if they were sometimes being watched in the museum by an unseen force, and have experienced random cold spots around the property.

The most commonly known ghost seen at the Egyptian Museum is the founder, H. Spencer Lewis, who passed away in 1939. The spirit of the round little man, dressed in '30s attire or fraternal regalia, has been witnessed in the front of the property or on the corner, waving to people as they pass by. The merry spirit has been witnessed over decades by dozens of citizens. Some who say they tried speaking to H.

Spencer claim that he smiled at them and then disappeared before their very eyes.

The Rosicrucian Egyptian Museum, San Jose, CA

The Planetarium is claimed to be the most haunted building on the premises. Eerie disembodied voices and cries have been heard on occasion. A female spirit is believed to haunt the building and has been heard crying uncontrollably. Her intense energy has filled the Planetarium at times, and many people have literally run out in fright.

A past director who worked at the museum during the early '90s claimed to have had several experiences in his office on the property. He first heard voices speaking to him and footsteps around the room. After weeks of experiencing this activity, one day the director watched as a foggy mist began to appear in the doorway. Slowly but surely the supernatural haze coalesced into an Egyptian figure. The two stared at each other for several seconds before the spirit vanished.

The Rosicrucian Egyptian Museum, San Jose, CA

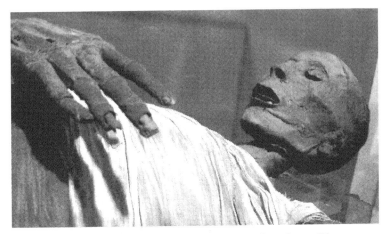

The Rosicrucian Egyptian Museum, San Jose, CA

Location:

1660 Park Avenue

San Jose, CA

~ 70 ~

The Sainte Claire Hotel

The Sainte Claire Hotel, San Jose, CA

The Sainte Claire Hotel is said to be haunted by a ghost bride who is claimed to have died on the property. In the early 1930s a woman by the name of Julia was to be married in the Palm Room at the hotel, until she was stood up at the altar by her fiancé. Unable to bare the pain and despair of her lover abandoning her, she allegedly hung herself in the lower level of the hotel in front of the elevators.

The 2nd floor where Julia allegedly hung herself, The Sainte Claire Hotel, San Jose, CA

Julia has been sighted in the hotel by several witnesses. In recent years, a couple photos that were taken in the Palm Room contained apparitions of the bride's feet and the train of her wedding gown. One of the Sainte Claire Employees claimed to have felt someone lie down beside him while sleeping in a bed there. Startled, he quickly glanced over to see who it was, and saw a white skirt and a woman's legs beside him on the bed. People have claimed to hear the sound of high heels on a hard floor walk past them in the Palm Room.

Where Julia's apparition has been seen, The Sainte Claire Hotel, San Jose, CA

A woman alleged having smelled a freshly lit cigarette in her room at exactly 2 a.m. on two complete separate occasions. She went out to the hall and noticed that the scent was not coming from there but from inside her room. She discovered that the smell was coming from a leather chair near her bed. 10 minutes later, the odor was completely gone.

I spoke with a manager at the hotel who claimed to be a total skeptic, until she had her first mind-boggling encounter in 2010. While the manager was making the last nightly rounds of the hotel, a spirit definitely wanted to make her become a believer. She said that as soon as she got to the second floor, she started to hear loud splashing noises coming from a hotel room.

"It sounded like someone splashing around in a bath tub," the manager said.

What was so strange was that the unexplained noise followed her from the second floor to the sixth floor, sounding as if it's coming from behind each door she passed.

"It seems like there's a lot of activity has to do with water", she went on.

Another employee heard water dripping deafeningly, while cleaning one of the hotel rooms. When checking the water faucets to make sure they were all off, the noise continued, but there wasn't water leaking from any source. The dripping went on for the rest of the time the staff member was in the room.

Additional Information:

- Most of the paranormal activity is alleged to occur on the second and sixth floor.

- Employees said papers mysteriously rearrange on their own and described feeling Julia's eerie presence in the office. Another manager witnessed a key to a cupboard fly off an upper shelf and smacked down in front of him on his desk.

Location:

302 South Market Street

San Jose, CA

San Jose State University

San Jose State originated in 1857 and is the oldest public educational institution on the West Coast of the United States. The campus is claimed to be haunted by several ghosts, but one spirit in particular is said to make an appearance during protests, rallies, or marches. Many believe that the "Phantom Protester" was once a well known teacher and poet by the name of Edwin Markham, who often attended school events for years before he died in 1940.

The ghost of Edwin Markham is described as an older gentleman in plaid pants and a tweed jacket and is witnessed walking with the crowd or standing quietly nodding his head. Some claim that when they first observe the professor at an event, they believe he's still alive. When they try and approach him, he is said to smile and nod, turns and disappears before their very eyes.

Additional Information:

- SJSU's Yoshihiro Uchida Hall was used as a processing site for Japanese internees during WWII. Students and staff members claim to hear faint cries and voices coming from the building.

Yoshihiro Uchida Hall, San Jose State University, CA, public domain photo

Location:

1 Washington Square

San Jose, CA

Trials Pub

The historic Victorian was built in 1894 as a hotel for railroad workers and is said to have been a brothel long ago as well. In the early 1900's the basement of the building was made into a small jail for the county because of the overflow of inmates at the big house. Many deaths occurred on the property long ago when the back porch of the historic building was used to hang convicts. It is said that an inmate was killed in a cell below as well.

The building was used by many different businesses over the years. In 1997 when Trials Pub was established, ghost stories began to arise. A past owner claimed to have had a couple unexplainable experiences when closing up one night. He and 4 employees heard the basement door, which is very heavy, open on its own. They were all startled when five human-like apparitions appeared on the wall in front of them. Another former owner claimed to hear strange noises around the pub while he was alone. An employee felt cold spots and also heard uncanny sounds. She admitted she didn't like to be in the pub by herself.

Trials Pub, San Jose, CA

Trials Pub, San Jose, CA

Additional Information:

- The apartment above the pub is said to have paranormal activity as well.

Location:
265 North 1st Street
San Jose, CA

The Winchester Mystery House

The Enchanting Winchester Mystery House was built around the clock from 1884 to 1922. The gothic Victorian was owned, designed and occupied by Sarah Winchester, wife of William Winchester, whose father invented the famous Winchester rifle. Sarah and William were married in 1862 and conceived a baby 4 years later. In 1866, their infant Annie died of a rare disease. Fifteen years later William Winchester died of Tuberculosis. Both of the deaths were traumatizing for Sarah and she lived the rest of her life in immense bereavement.

Sarah Winchester was always very interested in the paranormal and decided to see a psychic to help her grieve. She met with a medium from Boston who told her she was being haunted by the Indians who were killed from the rifles her father-in-law and husband produced. The psychic also explained that the spirits caused her husband and daughter's untimely deaths, and that she could be next. To save herself, the medium told Sarah to build a house out west for the Indian spirits to reside in. Trusting the psychic who she just had met, Sarah quickly bought an 8-bedroom home in Santa Clara Valley. She immediately hired carpenters to build non-stop adding more rooms to the house. In the end, it was transformed into a 7-story mansion containing 160 rooms,

2,000 doors, 10,000 windows, 47 stairways, 47 fireplaces, 13 bathrooms and 6 kitchens.

The Winchester Mystery House, San Jose, CA

What made the mansion even more unique was that Mrs. Winchester had the carpenters build doors to nowhere and staircases that lead to ceilings. She believed that these bizarre passage-ways would confound the evil spirits, in hopes that they would leave in confusion.

The stairs to nowhere, The Winchester Mystery House, San Jose, CA

Every night until her death, Sarah communicated with the spirits in her séance room known as "The Blue Room". At midnight she'd ring the bell in the tower to summon the spirits, and then she'd speak with them using the auto-matic writing method. During that time Sarah received from the spirits, instructing her as to proceed with the construction of the home. At 2 am, she'd ring the bell again to close the nightly channeling.

The Séance Room, The Winchester Mystery House, San Jose, CA

The number thirteen was very intriguing to Sarah Winchester. Believing that it signified good luck, she ordered parts of the property to be decorated and constructed in multiples of thirteen. She had her driveway lined with thirteen palm trees, had thirteen bathrooms built in the house, many ceilings had thirteen panels, and rooms had thirteen windows. She wore thirteen robes during her seances, signed her will thirteen times and even detailed the mansion with Chandeliers that had thirteen lights, thirteen hooks, thirteen drainage holes in a few sinks, and thirteen daisies, her favorite flower, in various stained glass windows.

~ 84 ~

Sarah would sometimes find bizarre traces of signs from the spirits and she took their warnings very seriously. One night Sarah Winchester went down to her wine cellar and discovered a black handprint on the wall. The spirits told her later that it was a print from a demon's hand. She was horrified and believed it was a word of warning to not drink alcohol. She immediately had the cellar sealed off with all her bottles of liquor still stocked and to this day it has never been located.

Sarah Winchester passed away alseep in her bed on September 5, 1922. After her death, it was believed by many that her spirit roamed the haunted halls of the sprawling mansion. Some people have actually caught a glimpse of Sarah Winchester at the Mystery House. Ghost Hunter and writer Antoinette May investigated the Winchester Mystery House with well-known psychic Sylvia Browne. In May's book titled *Haunted Houses and Wandering Ghosts of California*, she writes, "While sitting in Sarah Winchester's bedroom, Sylvia and I saw great balls of red light that seemed to explode before us."

Over the years, dozens of people have reported having paranormal experiences on the property such as hearing footsteps, chains rattling, whispers, organ music playing hammering, and feeling breezes and cold spots. There have been reports of smelling food cooking as well. Orbs are seen on the property, along with shadows, mystical lights, apparitions and door knobs turning on their own.

Sarah's bedroom where she passed away, Winchester Mystery House, San Jose, CA

Several people believe that ghosts of old employees roam the property. One ghost in particular has been seen on many occasions in the basement, dressed in white overalls, sometimes pushing a wheelbarrow. The ghost has also been witnessed walking up the stairs to the mansion and suddenly vanishing.

Annette Martin, who passed away recently in 2011, was a psychic from Los Gatos who claimed to have conversed with a spirit named Clyde on several occasions, who is said to haunt the Winchester Mystery House. Allegedly, Clyde told the psychic that he was a groundskeeper for Sarah Winchester and had promised to look over the property for eternity. Annette claimed that the ghost would meet her at the front entrance whenever she came to visit, concerned with the crowds of people going in and out of his boss' home.

The Author's brother, Jeff Jensen on the flashlight tour, the Winchester Mystery House, San Jose, CA

The Winchester Mystery House, San Jose, CA

The Door to Nowhere, Winchester Mystery House, San Jose, CA

Location:

525 South Winchester Boulevard

San Jose, CA

(408) 247-2000

www.winchestermysteryhouse.com

Agnews Insane Asylum

Originally known as "The Great Asylum for the Insane," many deaths have occurred in the Agnews Developmental Center, since it was established in 1888. On April 18th, 1906, over 100 patients were tragically killed in the San Francisco Earthquake, when part of the building collapsed. People have claimed to hear the screams of the innocent victims from the quake on foggy nights.

The Agnews Insane Asylum, aka Agnews Developmental Center after the 1906 earthquake, Santa Clara, CA, public domain photo

Many employees alleged hearing organ music playing late at night, along with the sounds of footsteps on the stairways. Doors were claimed to open and close by themselves, along with lights operating on their own. Ghosts had been seen on occasion throughout the Insane Asylum. One ghost was described as an old woman in a yellow dress begging people to help her find her children. Before the witnesses could reply, the elderly ghost would suddenly vanish. Another female spirit had been seen walking through walls from room to room and frightened one particular employee severely.

Additional Information:

- It is alleged that rooms would fill up with smoke, or strange smells, for no apparent reason.

- The building is now owned by Sun Microsystems and is no longer a hospital.

- At the time it was a hospital; another employee confirmed that it was common for workers at the Asylum to quit on the spot due to being uncomfortable with the ongoing paranormal activity.

Location:
4000 Lafayette Ave
Santa Clara, CA

Great America

Built in 1976, California's Great America is said to be inhabited by several spirits. A few people died at the amusement park, and it is believed by many that they haunt the vicinity. One ghost, who is said to haunt the premises, was a past employee who worked at the Roast Beef Shop. Years back, the employee got locked in the freezer and froze to death. It is claimed that almost every night between 10 to midnight, the ghost of the employee can be heard crying for help from within the walk-in freezer.

Both the Great America Theater and the IMAX Theater are alleged to be haunted. People have claimed to have heard their names being whispered in the Paramount Theater, and have reported feeling cold spots, being tapped on the shoulder, and odd noises and whispers. In the IMAX Theater there have been reports of lights turning on and off on by themselves, as well as eerie whispers.

Additional Information:

- A headless ghost has been seen near the entrance of the Top Gun roller coaster, late at night around closing. It scared two employees so bad they transferred to another area.

~ 92 ~

- Some say that the ghost of a boy haunts the ticket booth area after closing. Security guards have heard the cries of a child, but have never found anyone at the scene.

Location:

4701 Great America Parkway

Santa Clara, CA

Santa Clara University

Santa Clara University is built on an ancient Native American burial ground. At least 20 bodies of Ohlone Indians have been discovered underneath the school. The Mission De Asis is located on the University's property, and is also said to be haunted, as well as the bell tower and other parts of campus.

Mission Santa Clara, 1849, Santa Clara, CA, public domain photo

Built in 1777, Mission Santa Clara De Asis holds lots of history within its walls. The many deaths and traumatic events that occurred there long ago still haunt the property. Two men by the names of Father Jose Viader and Father Marcelo are said to haunt the premises. They resided at the mission back in 1814, near the time when hundreds of Indians lived there and died from various diseases. It is not said how the two men died, but allegedly their ghosts have been witnessed floating on the north wall, outside Santa Clara De Asis.

Additional Information:

- Ghosts of Jesuit Priests have been witnessed praying in the bell tower.

- Sounds of moaning have been heard from the cemetery located next door.

- Many dorms are said to be haunted at SCU. Several people have reported hearing doors slam when there was no one around accountable for it.

Location:

500 El Camino Real

Santa Clara, CA

Bella Saratoga

Bella Saratoga is believed to be haunted by three spirits who are said to have died on the second floor. The first death occurred in 1895, shortly after the house was built. Samuel H. Cloud, who was the first owner, ran into the street one day and unfortunately was hit by a car. He was taken into the front room of the second floor of the Bella Saratoga where he died. Samuel's wife Mrs. Cloud died in the same room years later.

Bella Saratoga, Saratoga, CA

The next owners began to notice unusual activity that they believed to be caused by the paranormal. Mrs. Cloud's ghost is said to haunt the building, particularly the women's restroom and the office, both of which are located on the second floor. She has also been witnessed climbing the staircase and standing at the top of it. Occasionally her ghost has been seen near the bar.

Samuel H. Cloud, 1890s, courtesy of Bella Saratoga, Saratoga, CA

The second floor of Bella Saratoga, Saratoga, CA

The staircase where Mrs. Cloud's apparition has been witnessed,
Bella Saratoga, Saratoga, CA

~ 98 ~

The third ghost, whom employees claim to feel frequently, is a spirit of a little girl. A previous owner of Bella Saratoga said that the little girl had also died on the second floor, while her mother was away. The girl's spirit wanders the rooms upstairs, endlessly searching for her mom.

Cold spots have been reported in the ladies' room, and water faucets turning on by themselves. Some claim to have actually witnessed the handle of a water faucet turning. There are accounts of strange noises being heard, doors and windows opening and closing on their own, as well as objects being moved or lost.

Additional Information:

- There have been reports of paranormal activity happening at the home for generations, long before it was a restaurant.

Location:

14503 Big Basin Way

Saratoga, CA

Madronia Cemetery

Originated in 1854, Madronia Cemetery is said to be haunted by numerous spirits. Ghost hunter and author Jeff Dwyer claimed to have heard both male and female voices whispering in the dark, while investigating the graveyard on several occasions.

"My first impression was that there must be a large group staging a memorial service by moonlight, but my search for other living souls has always turned up with nothing." Jeff Dwyer, *Ghost Hunter's Guide to the San Francisco Bay Area, Revised Edition, 2011.*

Dwyer received EVPs on his recorder, most of them about a minute in length. He explained that the spirits he overheard conversing didn't sound very intelligent, but did seem to be capable of carrying on animated conversations.

Madronia Cemetery, Saratoga, CA

Location:

14766 Oak Street

Saratoga, CA

The Hindu Temple

On August 21, 2006 news swept the globe about the miracle which started in India back in 1995 and manifested once again. Hindu Statues were consuming and drinking milk offerings from hundreds of people for up to three days after, until the phenomena stopped. Many skeptics were completely baffled when watching as the spoon full of milk disappeared within minutes.

The bronze statue that is said to drink milk offerings, The Hindu Temple, Sunnyvale, CA

This unexplainable miracle also occurred at the Hindu Temple in Sunnyvale. The stone statues of Lord Shiva and Lord Ganesha miraculously drank from the devotees for 3 days.

A shrine at the Hindu Temple, Sunnyvale, CA

When visiting the temple, I felt lots of spiritual energy within the building, and the air was very heavy. While observing the shrines, I wondered if any spirits inhabited the dolls or statues.

Location:

420 Persian Drive

Sunnyvale, CA

Toys "R" Us

In the 1800s, a wealthy landowner by the name of Martin Murphy Jr. owned a large orchard and abundant farmhouse where Toys "R" Us stands. Murphy hired a ranch-hand by the name of Johnny Johnson, also known as Yonny Yohnson, who enjoyed preaching in his spare time.

Johnny fell in love with Murphy's daughter Elizabeth, aka Beth and was heartbroken when she told him she was leaving to be married back east to another man. Beth's departure left Johnny devastated; he began chopping wood furious and fast. The axe slipped and cut his leg, and Johnny slowly bled to death; in the summer of 1881.

As soon as the toy store was built on the Murphy land, paranormal activity began to arise. Many people, including psychic Sylvia Browne, believe that Johnny is endlessly searching and waiting for his love Beth. Employees have claimed to have seen toys and boxes fly off of shelves, and find toys lying in the middle of the aisles when opening the store. Some have heard the sounds of horses galloping, unnerving whispers, sobbing and voices calling out their name. A number of people have also reported feeling breezes and cold spots throughout the haunted building. Some women claimed to have felt their hair getting brushed when no one was nearby. There have also been claims of lights turning off and on, electronic toys starting on their own and faucets turning on by themselves in the women's restroom.

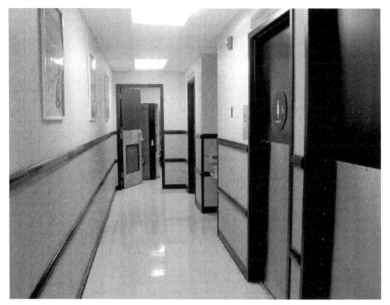

Where Jonny Johnson's spirit is believed to reside, the back hall in Toys "R" Us, Sunnyvale, CA

Staff members claimed to hear strange voices over the intercom, when there was no one near the microphone in the locked office. One night while employees were closing up, they all heard a voice say "The Lord giveth, the Lord taketh away." One employee reported seeing Johnny's ghost who appeared in knickers, a long sleeved shirt, and a tweed snap-brim cap.

Sylvia Browne conducted a séance at Toys "R" Us in 1978, which appeared on the T.V. show, *That's Incredible.* Sylvia claimed that as soon as she saw Johnny, she heard him say, "Have Mercy on me Beth." During the séance photos were being taken constantly with two different types of film. Johnny's full body apparition was captured on infra-red film, making it one of the rarest ghost photos ever taken. At that exact moment, another camera with high speed film took a photo, but Johnny didn't appear. This proved that it couldn't have been a human's shadow. As an employee shared in an article on www.forrense.com, "Funny things happen there you can't explain."

The haunted Toys "R" Us, Sunnyvale, CA

Recently, I spoke with a few employees as well as the manager of Toys "R" Us, who all believe Johnny's spirit still resides in the building. The manager said that a couple years back, a few guys were doing construction work upstairs where Johnny is also known to hang out, and left quickly without finishing their job, due to being scared by the ghost. Unfortunately, they didn't give any details. The manager explained that she wasn't sure about the toy store being haunted until she began to have encounters of her own. While walking down an aisle, a popcorn bag fell off the rack in front of her. She picked it up and put it back. As she started to walk away it fell again. She fixed it once more and heard it fall again seconds after.

"Okay Johnny," she said out loud, "... we'll just leave it there then."

The manager said that toys from the sports aisle are still being moved by Johnny during the night. When entering the store in the morning, it is common to find numerous sports toys sitting in the middle of the aisle.

In 2010, while the store was closed and locked tightly for the night and not one staff member was on the property, the front doors opened on their own. They stayed open for 30 minutes until the police arrived. When law enforcement and management watched the video recordings, they didn't see anyone in or around the building, and couldn't find any evidence that there had been an intruder. It was concluded by most that viewed the video or heard the story that it was Johnny who opened the doors.

Additional Information:

- Another employee believes she was pushed off a ladder by Johnny when she was in the attic.

Location:

130 East El Camino Real

Sunnyvale, CA

More Paranormal Hot Spots of
Santa Clara County

CUPERTINO

Homestead Highschool
21370 Homestead Road

- A ghost has been witnessed and felt on the 2nd floor. Doors are said to lock and open on their own. A teacher who worked at the school claimed to have felt the ghost tap his shoulder.

GILROY

The Old Gilroy Hotel
7365 Monterey Road

- It is alleged that the old hotel is haunted by a woman in her 20s who can be seen at the top of the stairs, and a little girl has been witnessed in the hallway and looking out the windows. Door knobs rattle, lights go on and off and the sound of footsteps has been reported. A previous employee claimed to have been touched by a cold unseen force on the back of his neck.

LOS GATOS

Borders Books

50 University Ave Ste 280

- The building where Borders Books used to be is allegedly haunted by a boy and an old man. Sightings of both ghosts have been reported.

MILPITAS

The Ed Levin Cemetery

Calaveras Road

- The condemned cemetery is known for its uncanny cries and screams that are heard throughout the night. During the day electronics are said to shut off or start up on their own, and people often have car problems. Cold spots are felt throughout the graveyard as well.

MORGAN HILL

The Golden Oak Restaurant
15595 Condit Road

- Several ghosts have been sighted in the restaurant by guests and employees. It is alleged that glasses have been witnessed jumping off tables, and an employee claimed to have made contact with the spirit of a boy by using a Ouija board. A strange high-pitched scream has been heard from the back of the restaurant, and two employees say that after closing one night, they witnessed a ghost of a woman standing on the roof singing. The scent of a freshly lit cigarette has been smelled when no one is smoking.

The Morgan Hill Times
30 East Third Street

- It is claimed that in the 1960s, a woman who was residing in the upstairs apartment died of a heart attack. People have reported seeing her apparition standing at the second story window.

Scramblz Diner

775 East Dunne Avenue

- Once an old Victorian home, the diner is claimed to be haunted by a poltergeist. There have been reports of the cash register opening on its own, and dishes flying off the shelves.

MOUNTIAN VIEW

Moffett Field

Off of Highway 101

- The Moffett Field naval base is allegedly haunted, and sightings of a little girl in Victorian era clothing have been witnessed at night by multiple security guards.

SAN JOSE

AMC Saratoga 14

700 El Paseo De Saratoga

- Employees and guests have claimed to feel a ghostly presence in the building. It is alleged that arm rests move on their own. This is most commonly witnessed in theater 5. A shadow-figure has been seen in the projection booth in theater 5 also.

The Bernal Gulnac Joice Ranch
372 Manila Drive

- The Ghost Trackers Association claimed to have heard the sounds of sticks tapping together throughout the bottom floor, as well as footsteps and disembodied whispers. They also heard the sound of cards shuffling in the parlor.

Del Mar High School
1224 Del Mar Avenue

- It is claimed that in 1942 a student was murdered by his best friend near the football field. For generations, teens have alleged seeing the boy's spirit run up the bleachers, and hearing screams coming from the vicinity at approximately 3 am.

The Dolce Hayes Mansion
200 Edenvale Avenue

- The ghost of a woman has been seen in the tower of the mansion, which was built in 1905.

Childlike apparitions have been observed throughout the halls. Disembodied voices have been heard and doors and curtains have been witnessed moving on their own.

Downtown San Jose

A private mobile home

- A home in downtown San Jose has been haunted for years. The owners, their family, and the current renter have all experienced uncanny events, such as seeing things move on their own. Years ago, a family member was videotaping his daughter in the home and saw the bicycle behind his daughter start to pedal on its own. The unexplained activity was recorded. In 2011, a renter claimed that the string hanging from the ceiling fan spontaneously started spinning hard and fast, when it usually hangs still.

The Late City Hall

North First Street – old location

- According to the book *Haunted Northern California*, 2009, during the month of December, "Merry spirits" are seen in front of

City Hall. They are believed to be the ghosts of the first legislators from December 15, 1889, when the first legislation was held there. Replaying that victorious occasion, the legislators have been witnessed dancing with glee in the late hours of the night, oblivious to anyone watching.

The Improv
62 South 2nd Street

- Unexplainable noises have been heard and orbs have been observed.

Mt. Hamilton Grandview Restaurant
15005 Mt. Hamilton Road

- Strange noises have been reported, as well as lights acting unusual. The ghost of a girl has been sighted on the patio.

Red Robin
1000 El Paseo De Saratoga

- The ghost of a child was caught in a photo sitting next to a girl in a booth in 2010.

San Felipe Road

South San Jose

- Legend has it; a white ghost truck appears out of the night and runs people off the road before disappearing. An old school house on San Felipe was supposedly condemned after a fire transpired. Many young locals claim that the building is haunted by children who allegedly died in the burn. Several ghost hunters have sprinkled flour or baby powder on their cars before driving to the haunted road. On returning, they find numerous child-size hand prints left in the powder on their car.

San Jose Skate

397 Blossom Hill Road

- It is said that long ago, a boy named Tommy fell into a dumpster full of water and drowned behind the roller palladium. His ghost is said to haunt the vicinity, and employees have witnessed eerie, dark shadows moving around after closing.

St. James Park

8 North 1st Street #1000

- People have seen apparitions of two men hanging from a tree at night or around dawn. The men were hung there by livid locals for kidnapping and murder back in 1933. The tree is no longer standing.

Quimby Road

Off East Capitol Expressway

- It is said that a man is seen jogging down the street at midnight. He is known as the Quimby Jogger.

SANTA CLARA

McKinley Road

Off Steven Creek Blvd

- McKinley Road in Santa Clara is said to be haunted by spirits. Residents claim to have witnessed ghosts wandering the area at night. One local alleged having seen apparitions in the road near Buy-th'-Bucket Restaurant. "I seriously don't like going over there," said the local. "It's that bad!"

SUNNYVALE

Quality Suites Inn

940 West Weddell Drive

- A man allegedly died of a heart attack in one of the rooms at the hotel and is claimed to haunt the vicinity. People have reported strange noises coming from the room when it is unoccupied, and ghostly apparitions have been witnessed throughout the hotel.

Alcatraz

Before Alcatraz Island was used as a prison, it was occupied by the Ohlone Indians. The Ohlones believed that the island was cursed by evil spirits who inhabited the area. The Indians also used the territory as a place for criminals to reside. Over the years many people died on the 22 acre land mass known as "The Rock" that stands a mile and a half off the shore of San Francisco. In addition to all the Indians who are said to have died there, records state that many inmates passed away during their stay at the penitentiary. Records indicate that eight people were murdered by inmates and five prisoners committed suicide. Fifteen died from natural illnesses, and seven were shot and killed when trying to escape. Two prisoners drowned, and five others vanished and are unaccounted for. Being one of the strictest and uncomfortable state prisons, as well as all the deaths, anger, rage and despair that occurred over the years, there's no question or doubt Alcatraz is inhabited by ghosts.

The most common paranormal activity that occurs in the penitentiary is unexplainable sounds. Footsteps throughout the halls and disembodied voices are heard as well. Security guards and employees have claimed to hear the sounds of someone moaning or crying, along with men's voices, whistles and screams. Many people have said that they heard a banjo being played in the shower room. It is believed that the music is played by the ghost of the legendary Al Capone.

Mug shot of Al Capone, 1931, courtesy of the United States Department of Justice

Part of Alcatraz has a confinement area where the prisoners were confined in a steel box in complete darkness for days to weeks. The incarceration boxes are known as the "holes" and are believed to be exceedingly haunted. Cell block

14D is allegedly haunted by a supernatural creature with red glowing eyes. Since the 1940s there have been claims of this eerie being having been sighted there. The sounds of screaming have been heard from the hole and many people claim that this particular cell is always freezing-cold even if the next cell over is warm.

People have claimed to see dark shadows move around the building at night. Others have said to have witnessed full-body apparitions. Two security guards claimed to have seen the face of the old convict who mysteriously died in the hole 14D when performing a head count. As soon as they recognized the deceased prisoner, he vanished. EVPs have been caught on location over the years at Alcatraz. When the famous team TAPS from the show *Ghost Hunters* investigated the island, they picked up an EVP from a former inmate. When asking whom they were speaking with, they heard a disembodied voice over the recorder say "Harry Brunette, 374," that was a former inmate that stayed at the jail for many years.

Psychic Sylvia Browne held a séance in the dining room after identifying the spirit of a convict by the name of Abie Maldowitz, known as "Butcher." Sylvia was able to see the ghost visually and encouraged him to go into the light and cross over, but he was in disbelief that such a place existed.

The spirit of Butcher is still known to haunt the penitentiary, particularly in the laundry room where he was murdered.

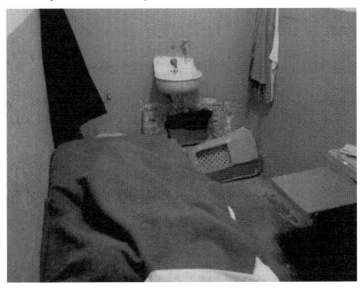

An Alcatraz prison cell with a chiseled air vent made by one of the prisoners who attempted to escape, courtesy of Wikipedia

Additional Information:

- Screams and cries are said to be heard often in Cell Block C.

- Strange clanging noises have been heard and the sounds of chains shaking.

Location:

Off the coast of San Francisco Bay, CA

The Bayview Hotel

The great, haunted Bayview Hotel was built in 1878 and still stands on Soquel Drive in Aptos. This amazing Victorian has been visited by many famous prominent people including Lillian Russell and King Kalakaua of Hawaii. The bed and breakfast hotel has had several different owners over the years and is operated as a hotel, bar and restaurant. It is alleged that in the 1860s, hundreds of people who died of disease were buried in one single grave located in the backyard of the Bayview.

The Bayview Hotel, Aptos, CA

For more than a century, spirits have roamed the hotel and formulate to make their presence known creating an abundance of disturbances and energies. It's well known that customers will up and leave in the middle of the night because they are scared out of their wits. I spoke and interviewed Christina, the Bayview's current owner since 2002. She affirmed that the Hotel is indeed intensely haunted, and that it would take her all day to explain all of her encounters with the ghosts who reside there permanently. Her first experience was the very first night staying in the hotel. She felt a cold gust of wind hit her and then smelled the scent of roses. Christina turned to where she felt the breeze in the hallway and saw an apparition of a woman standing on the other side of the mirror. Christina also encountered her bed shaking violently right before she would go to sleep, every night for 6 months.

Christina and her daughters, who live in the hotel on the third story, believe that visitors from the past must have passed away on the top floor. They may be the past owners who allegedly died there long ago. I asked Christina where the most paranormal occurrences happened and she verified that it was on the entire second level. The bar at the Bayview is known to have lots of paranormal activity as well.

The bar at the Bayview Hotel, Aptos, CA

A couple months before I visited the hotel, Christina's daughter had taken a photo of her refection in the hall mirror. When reviewing the photo, she noticed a hand coming from the opposite side of the mirror pushing out from the glass. All staff members, as well as the owner and her two daughters have had numerous accounts of paranormal experiences. Ghosts residing at the hotel are known to turn computers and televisions on and off, along with changing channels right in front of viewers. From stirring apparitions and dark shadows to faces, orbs, moving objects, disembodied voices, sounds and its very own graveyard, this haunted hotel really has it all.

Additional Information:
- Many have heard footsteps and singing in the halls.

- In 2000, a guest saw ghosts of what looked to be a mother and child in the bathroom.

- A ghost of a little boy is said to knock on the doors and has been seen looking out a window and suddenly vanishes.

- Previous owners claimed to also have multiple paranormal experiences including:

- being "waved at" by a ghost.

- A large framed picture gets tilted the same way every day.

Location:
8041 Soquel Drive
Aptos, CA
(831) 688-8654

The Brookdale Lodge

Nestled in the deep, dark Santa Cruz Mountains stands the famous Brookdale Lodge, built in the early 1900s. Recently renamed The Brookdale Inn and Spa, it is claimed by psychics and locals to be haunted by 49 spirits, who decided to never check out. It is also believed that there are portals around the lodge, allowing spirits to come and go as they please. Past owners hired several priests and psychics to try and rid the hotel of the disturbing ghostly visitors, who didn't seem to comply.

The most well-known ghost who roams the hotel is said to be a little girl by the name of Sarah Logan, the niece of the lodge's first owner James Harvey Logan. Little Sarah has been seen more than any other spirit in the lodge. The six-year-old slipped and fell to her death in the creek that runs through the Brook Room Dining Hall. Over the years there have been countless sightings of her spirit, by visitors and employees. She has been observed wearing a blue and white Victorian Sunday dress, near the fireplace in the lobby, or running throughout the halls and on the balconies of the Brook Room. Some claim to have approached Sarah and spoken to her, as she cried for her mother. When the witnesses looked away, she vanished.

Another ghost who has been seen by many is speculated by psychics to be Sarah Logan's Mother, who is believed to be looking for her daughter. Like her daughter, she is too mostly seen in the Brook Room. The smell of Gardenias often permeates the room at night, though there are no Gardenias throughout the entire haunted lodge. Several people who experienced the paranormal phenomenon believe that the smell is from Sarah's Mother.

The Brook Room has been identified to have the most paranormal activity of all the rooms in the hotel. Many have claimed to have heard glasses, plates, and silverware clinking, as well as footsteps, voices and conversations from dozens of ghostly diners. Some have even caught ghosts on film. Recently a couple ran out in fear after spotting a ghost in the background of one of their digital photos they were reviewing. It has been reported that the batteries of cell phones and cameras go dead quickly, from ghosts drawing the energy from any source they can.

The Brook Room, Brookdale Lodge, Brookdale, CA

The Brook Room, Brookdale Lodge, Brookdale, CA

The Pool Room is believed to be haunted by a 13-year old girl who allegedly drowned in the pool in 1972, forcing the pool's closure. Guests have complained about randomly feeling cold spots, as well as getting touched by unseen forces. Some claim to have heard the teen speak quietly and heard splashing in the pool when it was vacant.

The kitchen in the Brook Room is said by employees to have constant phenomena, from pots and pans swinging and banging around, to shadow-like figures that fly about. In an article from the Santa Cruz Sentinel dated January 9, 2008, a chef claimed to have seen a heavy cooking pot full of water do a full rotation on the burner. He said the doors to the kitchen swing open and closed, as if someone were walking through them.

The Mermaid Room is another hot spot in the lodge. Some have stated that they witnessed the ghost of a man standing at the bar having a drink long after closing. Visitors and employees have heard whispers, voices, clinking glasses and soft music when the Mermaid Room was completely empty. The jukebox is known to turn off and on and glasses and chairs move on their own. One never feels completely alone in this room.

At the bar there's usually a story going around about the most recent haunting that has taken place. Bartenders at the Lodge are aware that they don't just clean up for the living, ---

they clean up after the dead as well when glasses and bottles fly and slide off the shelves.

Additional Information:

-   Room 13 was changed to room 12 A because of complaints of activity. Room 49 is allegedly very haunted.

-   Many psychics have visited the lodge including Sylvia Browne who visits occasionally after she said she communicated with Sarah Logan's spirit.

-   Employees and locals believe that the hauntings have increased greatly since the lodge's recent change of ownership.

-   The Lodge has been visited by many famous people, such as President Herbert Hoover, Mae West, James Dean, Marilyn Monroe, Shirley Temple, Tyrone Power, and many more.

Location:
11570 Hwy 9
Brookdale, CA

The Golden Gate Bridge

Built in 1937, the Golden Gate Bridge is known for being the most popular suicide location in the world. Since the bridge opened, over 1,300 people have jumped to their deaths, falling 4,200 feet into the sea. It is claimed that on foggy nights you can hear the quiet screams of the people who fell into the darkness. Several people have claimed to have observed ghosts and apparitions on the bridge shrouded by the fog. They say they stand on the edge of the bridge and then suddenly disappear seconds to a minute later.

In 1853, a ship known as the SS Tennessee vanished in the strait, near where the bridge was later built. Since its unexplainable disappearance, the ship has been seen by countless people over the years. Some have said to have seen the phantom ship pass below the bridge and disappear minutes later. In 1942, a crew member aboard the USS Kennison saw the late SS Tennessee's ghostly apparition pass by. After watching the errie vessel fade away into the night, he noticed that it did not register on his ship's radar.

Location:

The Bridge that connects San Francisco Bay and Marin County, CA

Mission San Jose

Founded in 1797, Mission San Jose and its cemetery are claimed to be haunted and very active. The church was built on top of some graves, and many people have reported feeling cold spots and mists in the areas where the bodies lie. For years witnesses have seen "native-looking people" in old attire walk across Mission Boulevard to the house of worship, and disappear when they reach the courtyard of the Mission.

Many people have reported feeling cold spots on the steps of the historic building. Some believe that a ghost inhabits the stairs leading to the front door of the mission, faithfully guarding it for eternity.

The Mission San Jose cemetery next to the church is alleged to have creepy disturbances, such as ethereal sounds of crying and eerie whispers.

Additional Information:

- Strange energies have been felt near the fountain located in the court yard and uncanny mists have appeared there.

Location:
43300 Mission Boulevard
Fremont, CA

The USS Hornet

The USS Hornet was built in 1943 during the peak of World War II. During its service, the massive aircraft carrier shot down over a thousand planes and sank dozens of ships. Given all the blood that was shed on the ship, it's understandable that it would be one of the most haunted places in the world.

Soldiers at war on the USS Hornet, 1945, photo by a US Navy employee, public domain

Several former and current employees believe that the Hornet is inhabited by restless spirits. In 1998, the 900-foot long vessel was opened as a museum. People who were working on its restoration claimed to have had experiences with entities from another realm. Others deem there's residual energy left there from the war.

Many people believe that countless amounts of loyal spirits remain on the ship because of their strong sense of duty and dedication. The ghost of a marine guard, dressed in uniform with a rifle strapped over his shoulder, has been witnessed by several people patrolling the craft. Others have claimed to have had an encounter with a ghost of a friendly Hornet officer near the front of the ship as they'd come aboard for the tour. Some people discover he is a ghost after noticing his apparition wasn't in the photographs that they had taken.

A museum employee saw a dark, shadow-like apparition in the kitchen one morning. Later on, he went back to the area where he had seen the entity and started talking aloud to it. Within seconds a glass coffee pot flew off a high shelf, shattering on the floor next to him. That wasn't the only time an unseen force threw something at a worker in the kitchen.

In recent years, sensitive and paranormal investigator Nancy Bowman from Saratoga, CA investigated the Hornet with her ghost hunting team. Nancy had a couple experiences in an area of the Brig, where prisoners were held. While holding her tape recorder though the bars of a jail cell, an unseen force pushed her hand and bent it forward. In an adjacent cell, Nancy caught an EVP saying, "Help me... help." When investigating the hospital inside the Hornet, she heard a noise coming from one of the surgical rooms. When she turned around to see what it was, she noticed a bed with a large spot of fresh, wet blood in the middle of it.

Additional Information:

- Heavy doors slam shut and open on their own as well as the sounds of footsteps on the metal deck. Loud unexplainable tapping sounds can also be heard.

- Employees have claimed to have seen an apparition of a man hanging from a rope. It is said that the Hornet had the highest suicide rate in the Navy. Those who took their lives aboard the ship generally hung themselves.

Location:
707 W Hornet Ave
Alameda, CA
(510) 521-8448
www.uss-hornet.org

Glossary

Cold Spot: A small, defined area of intense cold that is at least 10 degrees colder than the surrounding area, believed to be made by a ghost when there's no natural or mechanical explanation.

EMF Detector: (AKA K2 Meter) A scientific instrument that measures electrometric fields. It is believed that ghosts give off electromagnetic energy which can be picked up on an EMF Detector or K-2 Meter.

EVP: (Electronic Voice Phenomenon) A disembodied voice heard through the white noise or on a recorder.

Dowsing Rods: (AKA Diving Rods) Two metal L-shaped rods that move on their own. The dowsing rods have been used for centuries to find rock, graves, water, and any type of body mass underneath the earth. When standing above an area with material below, the rods will cross. Paranormal investigators have been using rods for years to communicate with spirits. The entities are able to move the rods for "Yes" and "No" responses.

Ghost Box: A electric device that allows you to listen in between radio frequencies and communicate with spirits through the white noise.

K-2 Meter: A scientific instrument that measures electromagnetic fields. (See EMF Detector)

Orb: An energy anomaly normally seen in photographs or on camera and rarely witnessed by the human eye. The circular ball of light has been seen in a different colors and moving diverse speeds and directions. It is believed to be a form of a spirit in transportation.

Sensitive: Psychic, Medium.

Ouija Board: A board with letters and numbers printed on the top to which a planchette is moved across it by individuals. It is believed the spirits communicate by working through the people touching the planchette.

Vortex: A momentary doorway or portal to another realm that allows entities and other paranormal phenomena to come into our world.

Special Thanks To:

My husband, Sean Parola; Sensitive Nancy Bowman and Global Paranormal Society, (GPS); Bay Area Ghost Hunters, (BAGH); Lucy Rucchio; my Mom; Jeff Dwyer; the Sunnyvale Toys "R" Us; and the Bella Saratoga Employees.

Sources

Books:

- Dennett, Preston. *Supernatural California.* Pennsylvania: Schiffer Publishing Ltd.; 2006.
- Dwyer, Jeff. *Ghost Hunter's Guide to the San Francisco Bay Area, Revised Edition.* Louisiana: Pelican Publishing; 2011.
- Dwyer, Jeff. *Ghost Hunter's Guide to the San Francisco Bay Area.* Louisiana: Pelican Publishing; 2005.
- Graves, Aubrey. *Supernatural Santa Cruz.* Charleston, South Carolina: Createspace; 2011.
- Guiley, Rosemary Ellen. *The Encyclopedia of Ghosts and Spirits.* New York: Checkmark Books; 2000.
- Lee, David. *Haunts of San Jose.* Pennsylvania: Schiffer Publishing; 2008.
- May, Antoinette. *Haunted Houses and Wandering Ghosts of California.* San Francisco, CA: The SF examiner division of the hearst corporation; 1977.
- Stansfield, Charles A. *Haunted Northern California.* Pennsylvania: Stackpole Books; 2009.

Articles:

- Amable, Jody. "Top Ten Haunted Places and Spooky Urban Legends," San Jose.com; 10/14/10.
- Guzman, Isaiah. "Ghostbusters Scour Brookdale Lodge," Santa Cruz Sentinel; 1/19/08.
- Guzman, Isaiah. "Stirring Up Spirits," Santa Cruz Sentinel; 1/11/08
- Mickelson, Gwen. "Fabled Brookdale Lodge - - Ghost and all - - Up for Sale," Santa Cruz Sentinel; 5/17/07.

- Parker, Ann. "Spirited Dining at the Brookdale Lodge," Santa Cruz Sentinel; 9/14/05.
- Robinson, John. "Ghosts Said to Haunt Hotel," Santa Cruz Sentinel; 10/31/86.
- Tryde, Wendy. "Ghosts of an Old Hotel," Santa Cruz Sentinel; 10/31/00
- Villagrn, Nora. "Grand Link to Past," San Jose Mercury News; 2/14/2007.
- Walch, Bob. "Brookdale Lodge's Ghost Intrigues Tourists," Santa Cruz Sentinel; 10/25/07

Websites:

- http://en.wikipedia.org/wiki/Agnews_Developmental_Center
- http://en.wikipedia.org/wiki/Murder_of_Marcy_Renee_Conrad
- http://ghost-girls.org/invest.php?site=12
- http://ghosthauntings.org/Fords_Opera_House.aspx
- http://ghostsofhalloween.blogspot.com/2009/03/thats-incredible-haunted-toys-r-us.html
- http://gocalifornia.about.com/od/cahauntedplaces/a/toys_r_us.htm
- http://hubpages.com/hub/Agnews_Insane_Asylum
- http://phcal.com/cases/grant_ranch/index.html
- http://theshadowlands.net
- http://www.2010airportreservations.ca/stay-at-the-haunted-hotels-of-san-jose/
- http://www.associatedcontent.com/article/388898/haunted_sainte_claire_hotel_in_san.html?cat=37

- http://www.associatedcontent.com/article/5891644/spooky _ghost_story_in_san_jose_ca_pg2.html?cat=8
- http://www.bjwrr.org/
- http://www.daftmusings.com/2007/02/15/the-notorious-tale-of-san-joses-grant-family/
- http://www.ghosthaunts.com/grant_house.html
- http://www.ghostsofamerica.com/9/California_Milpitas_ghost_sightings.html
- http://www.gilroydispatch.com/news/80380-dont-get-spooked-on-pacheco-pass-highway
- http://www.hauntedbay.com/features/goldengate.shtml
- http://www.hoteltravelcheck.com/haunted-hotels-san-jose.html
- http://www.indolink.com/NRINews/mrclSval.html
- http://www.legendsofamerica.com/ca-alcatrazghosts.html
- http://www.morganhilltimes.com/news/171480-golden-oaks-ghostly-stories
- http://www.prairieghosts.com/gpalcatraz.html
- http://www.realtown.com/LiveInLosGatos/blog/hauntedlosgatos
- http://www.rense.com/general68/ghostsrus.htm
- http://www.strangeusa.com/Viewlocation.aspx?id=1091&t=5/12/2011%207:47:26%20AM&Action=Reply&CommentID=1592
- http://www.surfingtheapocalypse.com/unexplained 2.html
- http://www.ufofreeparanormal.com/node/78

- http://www.waymarking.com/waymarks/WM384N_Hotel_S ainte_Claire_San_Jose_CA
- http://www.weirdca.com/location.php?location=88
- http://www.weirdfresno.com/2011/03/haunted-pacheco-pass.html
- http://www.winchestermysteryhouse.com/sarahwin chester.cfm
- http://www.xprojectmagazine.com/archives/paranormal/hc _other.html
- http://www.yelp.com/biz/the-sainte-claire-san-jose#query:haunted%20hotels
- http://www.yelp.com/topic/san-jose-haunted-places-in-san-jose
- http://www.yourghoststories.com/famous-ghost-stories/winchester-mystery-house.php

Videos:

- Travel Channel's *Ghost Adventures*. Season 4, Episode 8: The U.S.S. Hornet: San Francisco, California. Aired: November 5, 2010.

About the Author

Paranormal investigator, empath, and conduit Aubrey Graves resides in Santa Cruz with her husband Sean, their two dogs and several lingering spirits.

www.aubreygraves.com

Made in the USA
San Bernardino, CA
23 September 2017